Rosie's Treasure Hunt

Peter Brownlow

Other books written by Peter Brownlow

The First Lamb

The First Frog

The Silent Wolf

Illustrated by Stef Parkinson

The Lost Rabbit

Illustrated by A. Fairclough

Panda Makes A Cake

All available at wilderswood-storytellers.myshopify.com and Amazon

Rosie, the black Labrador rescue dog from Cyprus, was on the hunt for treasure. She known there was valuable treasure somewhere about the house but she did not know where.

So, she set off to look for it.

But where could it be?

She soon came across two objects covered in mud and when she stuck her nose in one there was a horrible smell but they were just a pair of muddy wellies.

In the hallway something hanging from a hook was dropping diamonds that glistened in the sunlight but it was just water dripping from an umbrella that was drying there.

In the living room there was something gold on a small table which reflected the sunlight coming through the window but it was only a goldfish.

In the kitchen, which was lovely and warm, there was something that smelled delicious but it was not the treasure she was looking for. She would come back for some later.

In the bedroom there was something under the bed but it was something that had been in the muddy wellies. Pairs of smelly socks.

In the bathroom there was a bright golden glow from some candles around a steamy bath waiting for Rosie's human mum.

In the garden there was a patch of gold softly bathing in the bright sunlight but it was just a bed of beautiful yellow flowers.

In the garden pond there was a treasure chest on the bottom with gold coins and jewels spilling out of it. Rosie was not sure if it was some real treasure or just pretend.

In the shed there was some strange growling noise coming from the open door, could it be a monster protecting the treasure from those who what to take it?

Rosie crept slowly to the shed door and peered inside.

There was the treasure!

But it was not being protected by a monster, the treasure was making the noise and it was in the shape of her human dad, who was having a snooze and snoring very loudly.

Rosie treasured her human dad more than anything in the world. She jumped up onto his lap, waking him suddenly. When he saw it was Rosie he hugged her tightly while she licked his face and ears.

And the two of them spent the rest of the afternoon snoozing in the shed.

Life was better now that
she had been rescued.

She had found her treasure and
her happy forever home.

Rosie is a real rescue dog who owes an enormous amount of gratitude to the pet charity PAWS.

In July 2018, being less than a week old, she was found with her brother and sister, abandoned on a rubbish tip in Cyprus. There was no sign of their mother and PAWS took them all in and hand reared them into strong and healthy puppies worthy of a forever home.

With charitable donations PAWS was able to pay the vet fees and for the inoculations to allow all three puppies to come to the UK.

Their pictures were posted on the PAWS Facebook page and all three managed to each find a forever home in the UK.

Rosie continues to be healthy and strong, bring pleasure to her owners, Debbie and Peter, and enjoy a full and happy life.

Thank you PAWS.

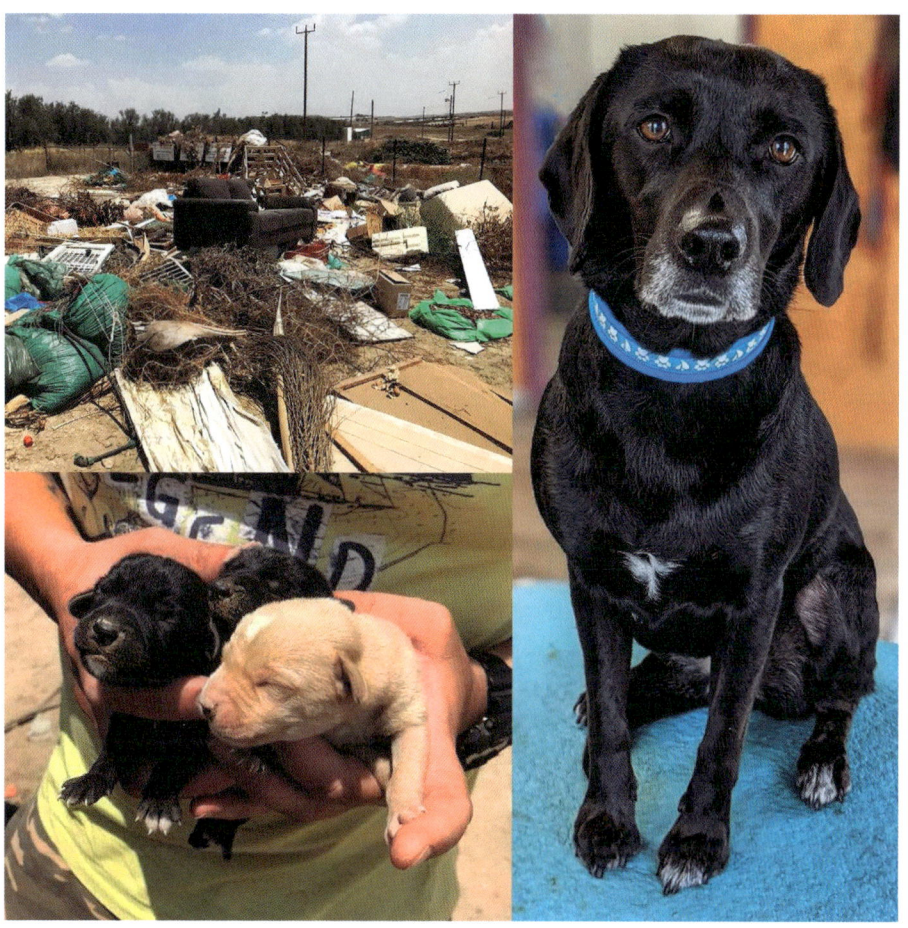

This booklet has been produced in support of the non profit-making pet charity **Protecting Animals Without Shelter (PAWS) Cyprus**.

It is the charity where I got my rescue dog Rosie from.

They rescue hundreds of abandoned dogs and cats every year and like all charities are in desperate need of funds.

If you have enjoyed reading this booklet and realised that there can be a forever home for all dogs and cats please consider making a donation to PAWS.

Donate through Paypal account "**info.pawscy@gmail.com**".

See their web page - **https://www.facebook.com/P.A.W.S.Cyprus/**

for more information or to adopt a rescued pet.

Thank you.

Printed in Great Britain
by Amazon

30888639R00025